Audiobooks & Voiceovers With AI

Turn Text Into Profit Using AI Voices for Audiobooks, Podcasts, and Narration Gigs

by Joe Correa

Published by Live Stronger Faster

This book is for educational and informational purposes only. The author and publisher are not engaged in rendering legal, financial, or other professional advice. Readers should consult a qualified professional before making any financial decisions.

First Edition

Table of Contents

Introduction

Over the past few years, something incredible has been happening—quietly, yet powerfully. Artificial intelligence has crept into one of the most human of all industries: the voice. Once, recording quality voiceovers or audiobooks required thousands of dollars in studio equipment, a trained voice actor, an audio engineer, and hours of editing. Today, all of that can be replaced by something you already have—a script and a laptop.

AI voice technology has transformed the way we create and share audio. What once took weeks and multiple professionals can now be accomplished in a matter of minutes, by a single creator using a few smart tools. And this book is your blueprint. Whether you're an author hoping to turn your writing into an audiobook, a freelancer looking for extra income, or just curious about how people are using synthetic voices to make money online—this is your guide to making it happen.

Imagine turning a blog post into an engaging podcast, an ebook into a multilingual audiobook, or a simple product description into a polished voiceover—all without ever speaking a word. That's the power we're talking about here. You no longer need a professional recording booth or acting talent. You just need access to the right tools and the right strategy. This book will give you both.

But before we dive in, let's answer a key question: *Why audiobooks and voiceovers? Why now?*

The answer is simple. Audio is booming. Audiobooks are one of the fastest-growing segments of the digital publishing industry. In the U.S. alone, audiobook revenue exceeded $2 billion last year—and that growth isn't slowing down. The convenience of listening while driving, walking, or doing chores has made audio content more appealing than ever. Globally, listeners are hungry for knowledge, stories, and connection—and they want it in audio format.

But it's not just audiobooks. Voiceover content is exploding across platforms like YouTube, Instagram, TikTok, and e-learning sites. Every time a creator uploads a how-to video, a brand publishes a product explainer, or a coach launches an online course, there's an opportunity for voiceover work. And here's the secret: most of that voiceover work doesn't require a human voice anymore. AI tools have leveled the playing field.

With tools like **ElevenLabs**, **PlayHT**, and **Descript**, you can create realistic, emotional, human-like narration in seconds. These tools offer everything from pre-built voices to full voice cloning capabilities—so you can replicate your voice or create a character with just a few lines of training audio. Want to create audiobooks in multiple languages? Done. Want to sound like a warm narrator or a dramatic storyteller? Easy. Want to add breathing, pacing, and emotion to match a scene? These platforms make it all possible.

So what will you learn in this book? A lot.

You'll discover how to use the top AI voice tools on the market, and not just how to generate audio—but how to make it sound amazing. You'll learn how to produce professional-quality audiobooks, create voiceovers for YouTube and podcasts, and sell your narration gigs on freelancing platforms. You'll learn where to publish your audio content to reach a global audience—and how to turn a single script into multiple income streams. Most importantly, we'll cover the legal side of things—what you can and can't do with AI voices, and how to avoid copyright violations or platform bans.

You'll also learn how to market your voiceover services, even if you don't have a portfolio or any clients yet. You'll see examples of creators who started from scratch and built real income online. Whether you're trying to make a few hundred dollars a month or build a full-scale audio publishing business, this book will show you the path.

Let's talk about who this is for.

This is for the **author** who's written a book but can't afford a narrator. This is for the **podcaster** who wants a clean, consistent voice but doesn't have time to record every episode. This is for the **freelancer** who wants to offer voiceover services without using their own voice. This is for the **entrepreneur** who's looking for a scalable, high-profit side hustle with low overhead. And this is for the complete beginner who's never used AI before but is ready to start something new.

You don't need a recording studio. You don't need a fancy mic. You don't even need your own voice. All you need is a script, a strategy, and the willingness to learn. The tools you'll discover in this audiobook are beginner-friendly, affordable, and incredibly powerful when used correctly. They allow anyone—from anywhere—to create and sell high-quality audio content in record time.

We are living in an era where the ability to speak, teach, or narrate can be automated. And while that may sound intimidating at first, it's actually the greatest opportunity we've ever had to scale our ideas, stories, and messages. It's never been easier to build a brand, a business, or a creative project powered by your words.

So if you've ever dreamed of publishing an audiobook, launching a podcast, or making money with your voice—but felt limited by time, money, or confidence—this is your moment.

About this Book

We are living through one of the greatest economic shifts of our time—and most people don't even realize it. Artificial intelligence is not just a trend. It's not a buzzword, a temporary wave, or a tech gimmick. It's a permanent evolution in how we create, communicate, and monetize our work. And nowhere is this shift more obvious—or more profitable—than in the world of audio.

This book exists because something incredible is happening right now: for the first time in history, anyone—regardless of experience, location, or budget—can turn simple words into professional audio content and get paid for it. This is more than a side hustle. It's a movement. A movement where text becomes voice, voice becomes value, and value becomes income.

Audiobooks and voiceovers sit at the crossroads of two explosive trends: the rise of passive listening and the rise of accessible AI tools. More people are consuming information through their ears than ever before. Whether it's on a commute, at the gym, or doing housework, listeners are craving content they can absorb while living their lives. And creators are racing to meet that demand—with audio content that is fast, flexible, and scalable.

The traditional gatekeepers of audio production—studios, agents, and recording contracts—are being replaced by tools that live in your browser. You don't need to be a trained voice actor. You don't need editing experience. You don't need expensive gear. You simply need a good idea, a clear message, and the tools you'll learn about in this book. That's why this book matters—because it gives you access to an entire industry that used to be closed off to anyone without connections or capital.

Let's talk numbers.

According to Deloitte, the global audiobook market is expected to surpass **$35 billion by 2030**, driven by younger generations, mobile-first consumption, and increased global literacy rates. Meanwhile, voiceover services are thriving on platforms like Upwork, Fiverr, and Voices.com, where voice talent is used for everything from video ads to explainer animations to audio-guided meditation tracks. The average voiceover gig pays between $50 and $500—and with AI, you can complete 10 of them in the time it would take a human to do one.

But that's just the beginning. AI voice creators are now monetizing in ways most people haven't even considered. Some are generating hundreds of dollars per day by turning blog posts into narrated YouTube videos. Others are creating multilingual versions of their books using cloned voices and selling them internationally. Coaches and consultants are repackaging their content into narrated mini-courses, meditations, or email responses—fully automated. This book doesn't just show you how to do voiceovers—it shows you how to build *systems* that run 24/7.

The potential here isn't just about making money—it's about freedom. AI narration allows you to multiply yourself. It lets you be in multiple places at once, telling your story, teaching your content, and serving your audience even when you're sleeping or on vacation. And because the tools are automated and scalable, your effort compounds over time. The audio you produce today can continue to sell or generate leads for years.

This book is also about *timing*. We're in a rare window of opportunity—a window where the tools are powerful but the competition is still low. Many people are hesitant. They think it's too technical. Too complicated. Too saturated. They don't understand that what used to take a team of professionals can now be done in a few hours with the help of AI. That hesitation is your advantage. If you act now, you can establish yourself while the market is still expanding. You can build your brand, your library, your client base—before everyone else catches on.

And let's not forget the global opportunity. One of the most exciting parts of AI voice technology is how easily it crosses borders. You can take a script written in English and generate it in Spanish, Portuguese, Hindi, or Mandarin in minutes. You can sell audiobooks in markets you've never visited. You can help clients narrate training materials, meditation apps, or podcasts in their native languages. You're not just building an audio business—you're building a global, multilingual audio empire.

Inside this book, you won't find fluff or hype. You'll find strategies, tools, and use cases that actually work. Whether you want to sell voiceover services, publish your own audiobooks, launch a faceless podcast, or just experiment with turning text into something more powerful—you're in the right place.

This book is divided into chapters that walk you step-by-step through the most important parts of this journey. You'll learn how to select the best tools, how to structure your content, how to price and position your services, how to avoid legal pitfalls, and how to market what you create—even if you have zero followers or experience. Each chapter ends with a story—real-world examples of people using these tools to build income, influence, or freedom. You'll see how everyday people—writers, freelancers, retirees, college students—are using AI voices to change their lives.

The future belongs to creators who embrace new tools early. Not because the tools are perfect, but because the opportunity is. With AI, you're not just outsourcing your voice—you're scaling your message. You're automating your creativity. You're reclaiming your time. And you're doing it all with minimal cost and unlimited upside.

This book will show you how to get started, how to scale, and how to succeed in the new world of AI-powered audio. And by the time you finish, you'll have everything you need to turn your words into wealth—and your voice into a business that speaks for you around the world.

So get ready. Because what you're about to learn can create lasting income, long-term freedom, and the kind of impact most creators only dream of. And it all starts with a simple script.

Chapter 1: Getting Started With AI Voices

The audiobook industry is exploding, and AI voice technology has arrived at the perfect time. If you're just getting started, it's important to understand the revolutionary potential of AI-generated voices and how you can leverage them to turn text into income. Whether you're interested in creating audiobooks, voiceovers for YouTube, narrations for courses, or selling gigs on freelance platforms, you now have access to tools that eliminate the need for microphones, studios, or vocal talent. This chapter will walk you through the foundational steps for starting your AI voice journey and monetizing your content, even if you've never narrated anything before.

To begin, let's break down what AI voices actually are. At the core, AI voice tools use advanced text-to-speech (TTS) engines powered by deep learning algorithms. These engines analyze patterns in human speech and replicate them in a way that is increasingly indistinguishable from real voices. Today's most powerful TTS platforms can simulate tone, emotion, pauses, pacing, and even regional accents. Unlike the robotic monotone of old-school voice systems like Siri or Alexa, modern AI voices can read an audiobook with emotion, deliver punchlines with timing, or sound conversational and natural enough to host an entire podcast.

There are a variety of AI voice tools on the market, but a few stand out due to their combination of realism, user control, licensing flexibility, and ease of use. One of the most popular tools is **ElevenLabs**, which is known for its ultra-realistic voice generation and emotion control. It allows users to select from a wide range of voices or even create custom voices by uploading samples. Another excellent option is **PlayHT**, which offers a fast, intuitive interface and supports multiple languages and accents. This is ideal for global narration projects or content that needs to feel native in various regions. For creators who prefer a podcast-like editing experience, **Descript** offers a tool called Overdub. This tool enables you to generate voice narration and edit your audio simply by typing. It also allows you to train your own AI voice using your voice samples, giving you full creative control.

Once you've selected a voice tool, it's time to start building your first project workflow. The key is to keep it simple at first. Begin with a basic script — this can be a blog post you wrote, an email you've sent, or a product description from your online store. Copy and paste the text into your chosen AI voice tool. Select a voice and preview how it sounds with your content. If necessary, adjust the punctuation or formatting to improve delivery. Many tools allow you to add pauses, inflections, or even specify emotions such as "excited," "calm," or "dramatic." Once the voice sounds natural, generate the audio file in either MP3 or WAV format. You now have a polished voiceover you can use in a video, podcast, or audiobook. Edit it in a free software tool like **Audacity**, or use **Descript** if you want to make changes by editing the script instead of the waveform.

A great way to build skill and confidence is to practice with short pieces of content. Start by converting a 30-second to 1-minute text into a narrated clip. This could be a motivational quote, a short blog post, or an intro to a YouTube video. These small tests will help you get familiar with the tool's controls, voice types, and audio editing basics. As you gain experience, you can gradually move on to longer projects like full podcast episodes, sales page narrations, or audiobook chapters. With each new project, you'll get better at script formatting, voice matching, and production flow.

While AI voices open up huge opportunities, you also need to be aware of the rules. Not all voice models are licensed for commercial use, especially if you're on a free plan. Some platforms require you to upgrade to a paid plan to use the generated voices in audiobooks or monetized videos. Additionally, if you plan to clone someone's voice — even your own — for commercial use, you must ensure you have legal rights and permission. Platforms like ElevenLabs and PlayHT often have consent forms or ethical usage guidelines in place to prevent misuse. Always read the licensing and terms of service before publishing or selling any AI-generated voice content.

Finally, let's talk about where this can go. Once you've mastered the tools, you can start turning your voiceover content into real income. You can publish audiobooks through **Findaway Voices**, **ACX**, or **Spotify for Podcasters**. You can offer narration services on **Fiverr** and **Upwork**. You can even use your own AI voice to create branded content for YouTube channels or courses. The key is starting with something small, mastering the workflow, and expanding from there. Within weeks, what was once a text document can become a library of profitable audio products, all narrated without you ever stepping into a studio.

Now that you understand how to get started with AI voices, let's step into a real-world story that brings it to life.

Alex and the power of ElevenLabs

Alex Martinez sat on the edge of his bed, staring at the glowing screen of his laptop. It was 2:13 a.m., and he was scrolling through freelance job boards, desperately searching for a side hustle. His day job as a customer service rep barely paid the bills, and his dream of becoming a digital entrepreneur seemed more distant than ever. Just as he was about to shut the laptop in defeat, an ad caught his eye: "Turn Text Into Audio. No Voice Needed. Start Selling Audiobooks & Voiceovers with AI." Skeptical but intrigued, he clicked.

The ad led him to a free tutorial about ElevenLabs. It claimed that with just a few clicks, anyone could generate lifelike voiceovers for audiobooks, courses, or marketing videos — no microphone or voice acting required. The idea sounded too good to be true, but Alex had always been a writer. If this could help him transform his old blog posts into audiobooks or narration gigs, it might be worth a shot. He signed up for a free trial, copied a section of a blog post he wrote last year, and pasted it into the script box. He chose a calm, American male voice with a touch of warmth and hit "Generate."

What came out stunned him. The voice was expressive, almost human. It emphasized certain phrases, paused naturally, and sounded like something you'd hear on Audible. He listened again, goosebumps forming on his arms. He hadn't recorded anything — just written words brought to life by artificial intelligence. Within an hour, he had created a 3-minute narrated sample that sounded like it had been professionally produced in a studio.

The next day, he uploaded his sample to Fiverr and listed a new gig: "I will narrate your script using a professional AI voice." He priced it at just $10, unsure if anyone would even notice. Within 48 hours, he had three orders — and one buyer asked if he could do an audiobook version of their eBook. Alex panicked. He had never made an audiobook before. But he remembered the tutorial mentioned Findaway Voices. After some quick research, he realized he could generate longer scripts in ElevenLabs, edit them in Audacity, and upload the finished chapters. That weekend, he delivered his first audiobook narration. The client left a five-star review and a $20 tip.

Encouraged by his early success, Alex created a system. Each morning, he would write or revise scripts. In the afternoon, he'd generate and edit audio. By evening, he was uploading samples, responding to client messages, and promoting his gigs. He added new voices, learned how to adjust tone and pacing, and even experimented with creating a clone of his own voice to build a personal podcast brand. Before long, his Fiverr profile had over 50 reviews, and he was earning more from AI voiceovers than his full-time job.

One of his favorite moments came when he narrated a meditation podcast for a client in Australia. The client messaged him, saying, "I can't believe this is AI. It sounds so real. My listeners love it." That message made something click. This wasn't just about making money. It was about helping people tell stories, teach lessons, and connect – using the power of technology.

Six months after that sleepless night, Alex handed in his resignation. He was no longer chasing gigs at 2 a.m. He had built a system that turned his writing into audio, and that audio into income. And it all started with one voice, one paragraph, and one decision to try.

Chapter 2: Choosing the Right AI Voice Tools

Now that you understand the potential of AI voice technology and how to get started, it's time to choose the right tools. This decision can shape the quality, licensing options, workflow, and ultimate profitability of your audio content. Whether you're creating audiobooks, podcasts, online courses, YouTube narrations, or freelancing voiceover gigs, selecting the best AI voice tool will save you time, improve your sound, and help you build a sustainable income stream.

The first factor to consider is **voice quality**. The realism of the generated voice is the most obvious differentiator between tools. Some free text-to-speech tools still sound robotic or emotionless. You want voices that convey tone, emotion, and conversational rhythm. Platforms like **ElevenLabs**, **PlayHT**, **LOVO AI**, and **Descript** offer near-human voices with the ability to adjust pitch, pacing, emphasis, and emotion. These are the voices that can sell a product, hold attention, and deliver long-form narration without sounding artificial.

Second, think about **use case compatibility**. Different tools are optimized for different types of projects. For example, **Descript** is ideal for podcasting and video voiceover because it allows you to edit audio by simply modifying the text. It even lets you remove filler words, background noise, and pauses automatically. **ElevenLabs**, on the other hand, is excellent for long-form audiobooks or storytelling, thanks to its emotion control and ultra-realistic delivery. **PlayHT** is best for multilingual content and quick turnaround jobs. It offers over 800 voices in 130+ languages and dialects, making it perfect for global audiences.

Licensing and commercial rights are the third most important factor. Not all tools allow commercial use of their voices on free or basic plans. If you plan to publish your audiobooks on Audible, sell voiceover gigs on Fiverr, or include AI voiceovers in YouTube videos, make sure you review the commercial usage policy. For example, **PlayHT Pro** and **ElevenLabs Creator** tiers offer royalty-free licensing, but only when you're on a paid plan. Using free versions for commercial work could result in copyright takedowns or worse — platform bans.

Next, consider **voice customization and cloning**. Some tools, like **Murf.ai** and **ElevenLabs**, allow you to upload samples of your own voice and clone it using AI. This means you can generate your own branded voiceover without recording every word manually. This is a powerful option for entrepreneurs, coaches, educators, and creators who want consistency across content — especially if you want to "be the voice" of your brand. However, cloning usually requires a premium plan and voice rights verification to ensure ethical use.

Workflow integration is another critical factor. Choose tools that fit into your existing content production pipeline. For instance, if you're using **Canva**, **Premiere Pro**, or **Final Cut**, check if the AI voice platform supports easy audio exports or plugins. If you're managing long-form content like e-learning or audiobooks, look for batch processing, chapter export, or bulk audio generation. Tools like **Speechelo** and **Synthesys** offer simple exports for video integration, while Descript provides timelines and multi-track editing for more professional outputs.

Pricing is the final but often decisive factor. Most platforms follow a freemium model, with basic voices or limited characters free, and professional use requiring a subscription. Starter plans can range from $9 to $29 per month, while higher-tier plans go up to $99 or more. Before subscribing, consider doing trial runs on multiple platforms and comparing output. The slight difference in quality or user experience could make or break your ability to deliver client-ready audio or engaging narrations.

To summarize, when choosing your AI voice tools, ask yourself the following: Do I need emotional delivery? Am I creating short videos or long audiobooks? Do I need voices in different languages? Will I publish or sell this content commercially? Do I want to clone my voice? And, does this tool integrate smoothly into my content creation system? The answers will guide you to the right platform.

In the next chapter, we'll walk through how to actually use your selected AI tool step by step — from writing the script to generating and editing the final audio product. But first, let's follow the story of someone who tested multiple tools, made mistakes, and found the perfect voice to build a profitable audio brand.

No mic, no studio

Jasmine Patel had always dreamed of becoming a storyteller. Her journals were filled with short stories, poems, and fragments of novels she'd never dared to publish. But life got in the way — as it tends to do. Between managing a small bookstore, raising two kids, and dealing with bills, her creative work stayed locked in folders on her laptop. That was until one Tuesday evening when she stumbled across a Reddit thread titled: "I turned my short story into an audiobook using AI — no mic, no studio." Curious and skeptical, Jasmine clicked.

The post linked to an audio sample created with ElevenLabs. Jasmine pressed play. A soothing, expressive voice narrated a paragraph about a post-apocalyptic world with such clarity and emotion that she leaned in. “No way,” she whispered to herself. “That’s AI?” She stayed up until midnight researching AI voice tools. The next day, after putting her kids to bed, she decided to test them out.

First, she tried a free web tool that promised realistic narration. It sounded robotic and hollow — definitely not what she wanted. Then she signed up for **PlayHT**. The variety of voices and languages was impressive, and she was surprised how quickly it rendered audio. But when she tested a story with emotional twists, the voice felt too flat. It sounded like a translator, not a storyteller. Not bad for quick narrations, she thought, but maybe not the one.

Next, she created a trial account on **ElevenLabs**. She pasted a few lines from one of her favorite stories and selected a voice labeled “Female — Calm & Expressive.” When she hit generate and listened, her heart skipped. The pauses were natural. The character’s emotion came through. The final sentence of her story gave her chills — and she had written it. “This is it,” she whispered. She knew this was the voice that could bring her characters to life.

Over the next few nights, she tested different voices for different stories. A deep male voice for thrillers. A light, youthful voice for children's tales. She even experimented with creating her own voice clone using samples recorded on her phone. It was surreal hearing herself narrate a story without actually speaking. With each tool, she took notes: PlayHT for international stories, Descript for her podcast idea, ElevenLabs for fiction.

But it wasn't just about the tools — it was about possibilities. Jasmine realized she didn't need to pitch publishers or rent a studio. She could narrate, edit, and upload from her living room. And so she did. She published her first AI-narrated audiobook on Findaway Voices. Then another. Then a serialized fiction podcast with AI voice actors. She marketed herself as "a new-age storyteller powered by AI."

Six months later, her books had thousands of listens. A small fanbase formed around her fantasy stories, some of them even writing fan mail. One listener from Germany wrote, "Your stories kept me going during a tough time. The voices feel so real." Jasmine cried reading it. What started as a Reddit thread turned into a career — not because she had the best equipment, but because she had the right tool and the courage to try.

Chapter 3: Creating Audiobooks Step by Step

Creating an audiobook with AI may sound like a technical challenge, but in reality, the process has been simplified so much that anyone with a computer and internet access can do it. In this chapter, we'll walk through the full step-by-step process of producing your own audiobook — from script preparation to voice generation, editing, mastering, and publishing. Whether you're adapting your own book or narrating someone else's content as a service, this process will help you turn plain text into a professionally produced audio product that you can monetize or distribute on platforms like Findaway Voices, Audible, or your own website.

Step one is preparing the script. If you already have a book or eBook written, this step is straightforward. However, it's crucial to review and format your text for audio. Written text doesn't always translate well when read aloud. Long paragraphs, complex punctuation, and overly formal language can sound awkward in audio format. Break your content into short, natural-sounding sentences. Add pauses where appropriate, use clear transitions, and adjust grammar to match spoken cadence. You want the listener to feel like they're being spoken to — not reading a textbook.

Next comes voice selection and narration using your AI voice tool. Choose the voice that best matches the tone and audience of your audiobook. For fiction, consider using a voice with emotional range. For non-fiction, opt for clarity, confidence, and warmth. Most platforms let you preview multiple voices with a sample script before committing. If you're working with a multi-character fiction piece, you may choose different voices for different characters. Tools like ElevenLabs and Murf AI support multi-voice output within the same audio file. Simply paste in your script, assign voices to the sections or characters, and adjust emotion or pacing as needed.

Once you've finalized the voice settings, break your book into manageable sections. It's best to generate the audio in chapters or subchapters to avoid large files and make editing easier. Generate each section individually and listen closely for pronunciation issues, awkward pauses, or audio artifacts. If needed, adjust the punctuation in your script or add "comma," "period," or ellipses to force more natural pauses. Once the narration sounds right, export it as an MP3 or WAV file.

The next step is editing and mastering. This is where you clean up the raw audio to ensure professional quality. If you're using Descript, you can edit directly by modifying the text and deleting filler words or repeated phrases. For more precise audio editing, use **Audacity** (free) or **Adobe Audition** (paid). Remove background noise if present, balance the volume across chapters, and add light compression to make the sound fuller and smoother. Make sure all chapters are normalized to the same loudness level, typically around -18 to -20 LUFS for audiobooks. This prevents volume jumps from chapter to chapter.

Once editing is done, organize your chapters in a numbered folder and create metadata for each file: chapter title, book title, author, narrator, and file number. These details are important when uploading to audiobook distributors like Findaway Voices or ACX. You'll also need a square cover image (2400x2400 pixels), a short description, author and narrator bios, and a rights ownership confirmation. If you're publishing under your name, you'll confirm that you own all content and generated voices or have permission to use them commercially.

The final step is uploading and publishing your audiobook. Platforms like Findaway Voices allow you to upload all your chapters, add metadata, and choose distribution partners — including Audible, Spotify, Apple Books, and more. You'll set a retail price, select royalty settings, and determine which stores you want your audiobook sold on. Approval usually takes 5–10 business days. Once published, you can start promoting your audiobook through social media, email newsletters, or paid ads. You'll earn royalties for every sale, often around 40%–50% depending on the distributor.

Creating audiobooks with AI isn't just a cool use of technology — it's a real business opportunity. With the right tools and workflow, you can turn any book, blog, or article into a product that earns you passive income for years to come. In the next chapter, we'll explore how to offer voiceover gigs for clients — but first, let's meet someone who turned her old blog into a bestselling audiobook using nothing but AI and determination.

Rebecca's story

Rebecca Lin hadn't touched her blog in almost three years. Once a weekly ritual filled with passion and purpose, her blog had faded into the background of her busy life as a marketing manager. But when her employer downsized during an economic slump, Rebecca found herself jobless and staring at the blinking cursor of a Google search bar. She typed: "how to make money with content you already have." Among the results was a video titled, "Turn old blogs into audiobooks with AI." It seemed oddly specific — and strangely perfect.

Intrigued, Rebecca opened her old blog archive. Dozens of long-form posts on personal development, mindfulness, and habit formation. She had poured her soul into these pieces. Could they really become something more? She copied her most popular post, cleaned it up for audio, and opened ElevenLabs. After testing a few voices, she selected one with a calm, grounded tone that felt like the perfect narrator for self-improvement. She pasted the text and clicked "Generate."

The voice was almost too real. It felt like someone else was reading her words — someone with confidence, clarity, and warmth. It made her writing sound even better than she remembered. She split the post into three parts and generated each as a separate file. Then she downloaded **Audacity**, watched a 10-minute tutorial on YouTube, and stitched the files together. The final product was her first audiobook chapter.

Inspired, she set out to turn ten of her best blog posts into a full-length audiobook. She created a simple intro script, generated it in ElevenLabs, and recorded her own name as the author and narrator using her phone. After compiling and editing each chapter, she followed a checklist: edit audio, balance levels, export files, format metadata, and upload. She designed a minimalist square cover on Canva, wrote a heartfelt description, and uploaded everything to Findaway Voices.

A week later, her audiobook was live — available on Spotify, Audible, and more. She posted a link on her old blog, shared it on social media, and emailed her tiny newsletter list. To her surprise, she sold 22 copies in the first two days. Not a huge number, but enough to make it real. The next week she sold 40. The reviews trickled in: "Soothing voice and helpful advice," "Listened while driving to work – loved it." It was validation she hadn't expected.

Rebecca started seeing her old content in a new light. She repurposed more posts, edited them into themed collections, and released Volume 2 within a month. By the end of that quarter, she had four audiobooks published, each earning a few hundred dollars a month. It wasn't a fortune, but it was consistent, passive, and growing. And most importantly, it gave her a creative outlet and an income stream during a time of uncertainty.

What struck her most was the realization that the barrier to entry had disappeared. No studio. No voice training. No team. Just her words and the right AI tools. What was once a dormant blog had become a branded audiobook series on personal growth – and people were listening.

One night, she received an email from a listener in Canada. "Thank you for sharing your words. I found your book at the perfect time." Rebecca smiled and closed her laptop. She wasn't just creating audiobooks. She was connecting, inspiring, and building something bigger — all from home, one chapter at a time.

Chapter 4: Selling AI Voice Services as a Freelancer

Now that you've learned how to generate high-quality voiceovers and audiobooks using AI, it's time to turn those skills into income. Freelancing with AI voice tools is one of the fastest, lowest-cost ways to start earning online. You don't need to speak into a mic, book studio time, or have years of experience in voice acting. With the right positioning, portfolio samples, and platforms, you can start offering AI voice services today and begin landing clients this week. This chapter will walk you through everything you need to know to sell voiceovers as a service — including platforms, pricing, profiles, delivery systems, and scaling.

Start by choosing your niche. While AI voices are versatile, you'll have more success if you specialize in a specific type of voice service. Popular niches include YouTube voiceovers, podcast intros, meditation scripts, audiobook narration, explainer video voiceovers, online course narration, voicemail systems, and radio ads. Think about the tone, style, and audience you're comfortable serving. Are you offering calm and relaxing voices? Professional and corporate? Energetic and upbeat? Your niche will determine how you market your services and what kind of voice samples you create.

Once you've chosen your niche, you need to create a **sample portfolio**. Even if you've never had a real client, you can create fictional projects that demonstrate your skills. For example, narrate a short script from a mock commercial, a motivational quote, a short story excerpt, or a course introduction. Use your chosen AI tool to generate clean, professional audio, then package those clips into a simple portfolio. You can upload the files to SoundCloud, Google Drive, or embed them into your freelancer profiles. Three to five voice samples, each 30 to 90 seconds long, is usually enough to get started.

Next, create your freelancer profiles. The best platforms for selling AI voice services are **Fiverr**, **Upwork**, **Freelancer.com**, and **PeoplePerHour**. Fiverr is ideal for beginners because it's easy to rank gigs with low initial pricing. Upwork offers higher-paying long-term clients but requires a strong proposal. On Fiverr, create a gig title like: "I will record professional AI voiceovers for your videos and audiobooks." Add relevant keywords like "voiceover," "audiobook," "narration," and "AI voice." Upload your samples, write a compelling description, and offer basic, standard, and premium packages based on word count or delivery speed.

Pricing your services depends on your target clients and experience level. A great entry point is $10–$20 for up to 100 words, $30–$50 for 500 words, and $75–$100+ for longer scripts or commercial use. Offer quick delivery for an extra fee, include revisions as a bonus, and upsell extras like background music or script proofreading. Keep your communication professional, deliver on time, and always exceed expectations — that's how you get repeat clients and five-star reviews.

As you gain traction, you can start scaling your business by creating systems. Batch generate voiceovers for multiple clients using your saved templates and voice settings. Use spreadsheets or a free CRM to track client orders, deadlines, and revisions. Create repeatable templates for responses, delivery messages, and proposals. As orders grow, consider outsourcing script formatting or editing so you can focus on sales and fulfillment.

Promotion is another way to grow quickly. Share your Fiverr gigs on social media, YouTube, LinkedIn, or in content creator forums. Create TikTok videos showing your AI voice demos and behind-the-scenes process. Reach out to content creators on YouTube or course platforms and offer to voice their content for free in exchange for a testimonial. You'll be surprised how many creators would love a professional voice without having to record it themselves.

Freelancing with AI voices is not just about earning income – it's also a gateway to bigger opportunities. As you build your client base, you can transition into producing audiobooks, creating voice-powered apps, or even licensing your own AI-narrated content. The demand for voice is everywhere – and with AI, you're never limited by your own vocal cords.

Now let's meet someone who went from being an unemployed student to a full-time AI voice freelancer using just a laptop, free tools, and a Fiverr gig.

AI voiceovers with Daniel.

Daniel Cruz was a 21-year-old university dropout with a laptop, no job, and a bank account barely above zero. He had always been good with tech, but after dropping out due to tuition costs, he felt lost. He didn't want a typical 9-to-5. He wanted to build something online – something that could give him control over his time and income. One day, while scrolling YouTube for side hustle ideas, he saw a video titled: "Make $100/day with AI Voiceovers on Fiverr." The guy in the video claimed he used an AI tool to generate voiceovers and sold them as freelance gigs. Daniel had never thought about selling voiceovers, but he figured it was worth a shot.

That afternoon, he signed up for ElevenLabs and created a free Fiverr account. He wrote a short script for a fake commercial

— a motivational quote paired with upbeat music. He tested different voices, tweaked the emotion settings, and generated the audio. It sounded shockingly good. He uploaded the clip as a sample and published a gig: "I will create professional AI voiceovers for your YouTube channel or audiobook." He priced his basic package at $15 and offered delivery within 24 hours.

Three days passed with no activity. Then, a notification. "You have a new order." A YouTuber wanted a 60-second video intro voiced. Daniel got to work. He asked for the script, chose a clear, friendly voice, generated the audio, and used Audacity to clean up the file. He delivered it within 6 hours. The buyer left a 5-star review. That review led to three more orders. Then five. Then ten.

Within a month, Daniel had completed 40 orders. He created new gigs for audiobook narration, podcast intros, and meditation voiceovers. He added upsells: faster delivery, commercial rights, background music. He reinvested the money into upgrading to ElevenLabs' paid plan and bought headphones and a simple editing tool. Every evening, he generated voiceovers in batches, edited the files, delivered to clients, and responded to messages.

He began getting return clients. A meditation coach from Bali. A YouTube finance channel. An author who needed someone to narrate all four of her books. Daniel realized that while others were struggling to break into freelancing, he had found a sweet spot — a service that was high in demand, low in competition, and required no vocal talent of his own.

One day, a client asked, "Do you also offer multilingual voiceovers?" Daniel did some research and added **PlayHT** to his toolkit. Now he could offer Spanish, Portuguese, and French voiceovers too. That opened up new international markets. His income doubled. He was now making $3,000/month — more than any job he'd ever had. And it all started with a free AI tool and a voice that wasn't even his.

Daniel eventually built a team of freelancers to handle editing and script polishing. He focused on scaling — building relationships, creating systems, and marketing his services. He even launched a YouTube channel teaching others how to start their own AI voiceover side hustles. He wasn't just a freelancer anymore. He was running a digital agency powered by AI.

Looking back, Daniel often said, "I never thought I'd get paid to say nothing." But the truth was, he was saying a lot — through technology, creativity, and persistence. And with every voiceover he delivered, he proved that the voice of the future didn't need to come from your throat — just from your vision.

Chapter 5: Monetizing Podcasts, Courses, and YouTube With AI Voices

Beyond audiobooks and freelance services, one of the most lucrative uses for AI voice technology is in creating and monetizing your own content — specifically podcasts, online courses, and YouTube videos. Each of these platforms provides scalable, repeatable opportunities for generating passive or recurring income using voice-driven content. You no longer need a high-end studio or expensive gear to build a brand and income stream. With AI, all you need is a script, the right voice, and a monetization strategy. This chapter will show you how to turn AI narration into content that earns you money long after it's published.

Let's start with **podcasting**. Podcasts have exploded in popularity, and more creators are entering the space every day. With AI voice tools, you can now launch a solo podcast in any niche — even if you hate the sound of your own voice or don't want to record yourself at all. Choose a podcast topic you're passionate about or knowledgeable in. It could be personal development, entrepreneurship, storytelling, finance, relationships, or even AI tools themselves. Write short 5–10 minute scripts for each episode. Use a consistent AI voice to build familiarity with listeners, and generate your episodes weekly or in bulk.

Once you have your podcast audio files, you can publish through platforms like **Spotify for Podcasters**, **Buzzsprout**, **Podbean**, or **Anchor**. These platforms distribute your podcast to major players like Spotify, Apple Podcasts, and Google Podcasts. Monetization can come from sponsored segments, affiliate links in the show notes, listener donations through platforms like Buy Me a Coffee, or your own digital products and services. As your podcast grows, your AI voice becomes the consistent, reliable "host," and your income grows with every episode published.

Next, we have **online courses**. E-learning is a booming industry worth billions annually, and creators are earning significant income teaching what they know. With AI voices, you can now create high-quality narrated lessons without ever recording yourself. Pick a course topic — something you know well or are willing to research. Break the topic into short lessons or modules, each with a focused learning outcome. Write the scripts for each lesson, use AI voices to narrate them, and pair them with slides created in Canva or PowerPoint. Export the slides and narration as a video using free tools like **Pictory**, **Synthesia**, or **Lumen5**.

Once your video lessons are ready, upload them to platforms like **Udemy**, **Teachable**, **Thinkific**, or **Skool**. You can also sell courses directly using **Gumroad** or **Podia**. These platforms allow you to charge anywhere from $10 to $500+ depending on the course value and audience. Add AI-generated quizzes or summaries to increase engagement. The key is to automate and standardize the content, so your course runs on autopilot while you collect reviews and income over time.

Now let's talk about **YouTube**, one of the most powerful platforms for building a brand and generating passive income. Using AI voices, you can create faceless YouTube videos that earn ad revenue, affiliate commissions, and promote your products. Start by choosing a content niche like productivity, AI tools, finance, storytelling, or top 10 lists. Write short scripts for 3–10 minute videos. Use AI voice tools like **ElevenLabs**, **PlayHT**, or **Murf AI** to narrate the scripts. Add visuals using tools like **Pictory**, **InVideo**, **CapCut**, or **Canva Pro**. These tools let you drag and drop stock footage, animations, and motion text synced to your voiceover.

Once your videos are done, publish consistently and optimize them for search. Use strong titles, high-CTR thumbnails, and keyword-rich descriptions. Monetization comes from **YouTube AdSense** (once you hit 1,000 subscribers and

4,000 watch hours), but also from affiliate links in your video descriptions. Promote products, services, or even your own audiobook or course. You can also create paid memberships or offer digital downloads using platforms like **Ko-fi** or **Patreon**.

What makes AI voice content powerful on all three platforms — podcasting, courses, and YouTube — is its scalability. You can produce content faster than ever, experiment across different formats, and build multiple income streams without burning out. Start with one episode, lesson, or video per week. Focus on quality and clarity. Let the AI do the talking while you handle the strategy and monetization.

Next, let's follow a creator who started with zero followers and no camera but used AI voice tools to build three content-based income streams from home — all while staying completely faceless.

Cloe's story

Chloe Nguyen had never liked being on camera. She wasn't shy exactly — she just valued her privacy. While her friends were busy making TikToks and Reels, Chloe preferred writing. But she still dreamed of building something online — something passive, scalable, and meaningful. She had dabbled in blogging and affiliate marketing with little success. Then one day, while researching side hustles, she stumbled on a YouTube channel called "Faceless Creators." It featured creators using AI voices to make content that earned real income. That night, Chloe decided to give it a try.

She started with podcasting. Chloe had always loved talking about mental health and mindfulness. She wrote a 500-word script on "Overcoming Negative Self-Talk" and used ElevenLabs to generate a calming, warm female voice to narrate it. It was perfect — intimate, gentle, and professional. She added soft ambient music, exported the MP3, and published her first episode on Spotify using Anchor. No photo, no face, just her words and a digital voice. She promoted the episode in a few Facebook groups. To her surprise, she got a few messages thanking her for the content. One woman wrote, "Your voice feels like a hug." Chloe smiled — the voice wasn't hers, but the words were.

Encouraged, she created a second episode. Then a third. After a few weeks, she had a small but growing audience. She added a Ko-fi link to accept tips. People donated. Then someone asked, "Do you have a course on this?" That sparked a new idea. Chloe took her best podcast episodes and turned them into a course called "Reprogram Your Mindset in 10 Days." She wrote scripts, used AI voices to narrate each lesson, and built slides in Canva. She published it on Gumroad and offered it for $29.

Sales trickled in. Five in the first week. Then ten. Then someone shared it in a community group, and sales spiked. Chloe added a bonus guided meditation — again, voiced with AI — and increased the price to $49. She had made more money from that course in two weeks than she had in six months of blogging. The best part? It required no recording equipment, no video shoots, and no speaking on camera.

But Chloe wasn't done. She took the same content and created a YouTube channel. Using Pictory, she turned each script into a short video with stock footage and AI narration. She uploaded weekly: motivational content, mental health tips, calming visual meditations. She optimized titles, crafted thumbnails in Canva, and shared each video in niche forums. Slowly but surely, subscribers grew. After six months, she hit 1,000 subscribers and 4,000 watch hours — enough to monetize with YouTube ads.

Today, Chloe earns passive income from all three platforms. Her podcast brings in donations and builds an audience. Her course sells on autopilot through Gumroad and affiliate promotions. Her YouTube channel earns from ads and affiliate links for journaling tools and self-help books. All of it, built around her words and an AI voice.

She still hasn't shown her face. But her digital voice — that calming AI narrator she customized and made her own — is recognized by thousands of followers around the world. Chloe proved that in the age of AI, you don't need to be loud, flashy, or famous to build something impactful. You just need a message worth sharing — and the right tools to give it a voice.

Chapter 6: Building a Passive Income System With Voice Content

Now that you've created content with AI voices and learned how to monetize across multiple platforms, it's time to put everything together into a **passive income system**. A passive income system is a set of automated or semi-automated processes that continue to generate revenue with minimal day-to-day effort. Instead of always chasing clients or one-time gigs, this approach lets you create once and earn continuously from digital products powered by AI narration. In this chapter, we'll walk through how to set up your passive income machine using your voice content across multiple platforms.

The foundation of any passive system is **leveraging one piece of content across many income streams**. Let's say you've written a 10-page guide on productivity. You can narrate it using an AI voice and release it as an audiobook on Findaway Voices. Then you can break that same script into 5 podcast episodes using Spotify for Podcasters. Next, turn it into a mini online course on Gumroad. Finally, convert each section into a short faceless video for YouTube. From just one script, you now have four pieces of content across four monetized platforms — all using AI voice generation and free or low-cost tools.

The second component is **automating content creation and distribution**. Use AI tools to reduce how much time you spend writing, editing, and publishing. For scripting, tools like **ChatGPT**, **Jasper**, or **Claude** can help you quickly create outlines, blog posts, or lesson plans. Use AI voice tools like **ElevenLabs** to generate audio, and video creation platforms like **Pictory**, **InVideo**, or **Lumen5** to combine visuals with narration. You can even automate publishing using tools like **Zapier** or **Make.com**, where uploading a podcast episode can trigger social media posts or newsletter sends. This automation lets you keep publishing consistently without manually handling every step.

Next, you need a **central content hub**. This could be a website, blog, or link-in-bio page where all of your voice-powered content is accessible. Use a free website builder like **Carrd**, **WordPress**, or **Notion** to showcase your audiobook links, podcast episodes, YouTube videos, and courses. Add opt-in forms using platforms like **MailerLite** or **ConvertKit** so you can collect email addresses from fans and notify them when you release new content. Over time, this hub becomes the place where people find your work, engage with your content, and buy your digital products — all while you sleep.

Another critical element is **recurring monetization**. While one-time product sales are great, subscription models, affiliate commissions, and ad revenue bring long-term income. For example, you can create a subscription podcast using platforms like **Supercast** or offer paid digital content through **Patreon**. You can recommend AI tools or niche products using affiliate platforms like **PartnerStack**, **Impact**, or **Gumroad Affiliates**. And you can monetize your YouTube or Spotify content with ads as your audience grows. With the right structure, your AI-narrated content works like a sales rep that earns for you 24/7.

Don't forget to build systems for **promotion and visibility**. Even great content won't earn passive income if no one sees it. Schedule regular posts to Instagram, YouTube Shorts, TikTok, or Pinterest using your AI voice clips. Repurpose your podcast or video quotes into carousel posts or tweet threads. Use hashtags strategically. Engage with relevant creators. Build partnerships. And always include strong calls-to-action — whether it's "Buy my audiobook," "Join my course," or "Support my channel." Over time, your content becomes a magnet, pulling in new customers and fans without you having to sell directly.

Lastly, measure and improve. Use analytics dashboards from Spotify, YouTube, Gumroad, and Findaway to see what content performs best. Focus more time on what's working and cut what isn't. Test different voices, titles, and thumbnails. Optimize your scripts with emotional hooks and keywords. Over 6–12 months, your library of passive content compounds. You'll go from earning a few dollars here and there to stacking consistent monthly income — all from voice content powered by AI.

Now let's look at how one creator systemized his entire content workflow, built a five-figure income in under a year, and never recorded a single word with his own voice.

How Leo automated his way to $4,000 per month

Leo Ramirez had always been a systems guy. As a former IT analyst, he loved flowcharts, templates, and automation. But when he lost his job during company downsizing, systems couldn't pay the bills — at least not right away. He started freelancing but found himself burning out from constant client work. Then he stumbled across an article about "passive income with AI content." It sounded like a buzzword gimmick, but something clicked: "What if I used my tech skills to create content systems instead of trading time for money?"

Leo decided to test the idea. He wrote a short 2,000-word guide on time management and used ChatGPT to clean it up. Then, he fed the script into ElevenLabs and generated narration using a crisp, professional male voice. Next, he broke the audio into five segments and created a podcast using Spotify for Podcasters. He repackaged the same audio with slide visuals using Pictory and uploaded the videos to a new faceless YouTube channel. Then, using Canva and Gumroad, he bundled the content into a mini-course and listed it for $27.

All of this was done in a week.

But Leo didn't stop there. He created a Notion dashboard where he tracked each piece of content and where it had been published. He set up Zapier automations so every time he uploaded a new podcast episode, it would post to Twitter, Facebook, and his newsletter. He built a simple Carrd site as a central hub and added links to his course, YouTube channel, and podcast. Then he created templates for scripts, lesson outlines, thumbnail designs, and publishing checklists — all stored in Google Drive.

By the end of the first month, Leo had created five voice-powered mini-courses, a podcast with 12 episodes, and 10 YouTube videos. His YouTube channel had just 200 subscribers, but one video started getting traction. His course sold 13 copies. His podcast got 400 plays. It wasn't much, but it was happening — all from work he'd done once.

Over the next three months, Leo duplicated the system. He created new content in productivity, side hustles, and personal development — using the same workflows, the same AI tools, and the same voice. He started offering a bundle of his courses for $97. His YouTube channel reached 1,000 subscribers, allowing him to earn ad revenue. His email list passed 1,500 people. Everything was connected: his podcast fed his YouTube, his YouTube promoted his course, his course led to affiliate sales. It was a self-sustaining machine.

By month six, Leo was earning over $4,000/month — all passive. No clients. No calls. No custom work. Just systems, content, and AI voices working around the clock.

Leo's story isn't about luck — it's about leverage. He didn't have a massive audience or fancy equipment. He had a system, a strategy, and a willingness to automate what most people try to hustle manually. As he often said, "Build once, sell forever. That's the power of passive voice."

Chapter 7: Scaling With Voice Cloning, Multilingual Content, and Licensing

Once you've created your first few AI-narrated products and set up a passive income system, the next logical step is scaling — reaching more audiences, increasing content production, and multiplying your income streams. Three powerful strategies will help you expand: **voice cloning**, **multilingual content**, and **licensing your audio assets**. These advanced techniques can help you grow your digital business without burning out, while positioning you as a global content creator or even a micro-media company.

Let's start with **voice cloning** — the ability to create a custom AI voice model based on a real human voice. Most platforms like **ElevenLabs**, **PlayHT**, and **Resemble AI** now offer this feature. Voice cloning allows you to maintain brand consistency across all your content without manually recording. You can upload short samples of your own voice (or someone else's, with legal permission), and the tool will replicate tone, pacing, and inflection. This is especially valuable if you're building a branded voice for your YouTube channel, podcast, or audiobook series. Once you've cloned a voice, you can generate content at scale without compromising uniqueness or authenticity.

Voice cloning also allows you to build character-driven content. Imagine cloning a specific voice for your meditation series, a different one for your children's stories, and another for your business podcasts. This gives your content depth, variety, and personalization – which increases engagement and listener loyalty. Just remember, ethical use is critical. Never clone someone else's voice without consent, and always follow the platform's licensing rules.

The next level of scaling is **multilingual content**. With AI voice tools now offering realistic voiceovers in 20, 50, or even 100+ languages, your content can reach a global audience overnight. Platforms like **LOVO AI**, **Synthesys**, **Murf**, and **PlayHT** allow you to translate your text, select a native-sounding voice in a new language, and generate audio within minutes. You don't need to speak the language – just translate your script using tools like **DeepL** or **Google Translate**, review it with a native speaker (if possible), and narrate it using AI.

By offering the same audiobook, podcast, or video in multiple languages, you instantly multiply your market. For example, a self-help audiobook in English may perform decently in the U.S. and U.K. – but once translated and narrated in Spanish, Portuguese, Hindi, or Mandarin, it can reach millions more across Latin America, India, and China. Even if you start with just Spanish or French, you're tapping into massive non-English-speaking markets that are underserved in terms of digital products and audio learning.

Finally, let's talk about **licensing your AI-generated content**. Once you've created a library of high-quality narrated audio — whether it's meditations, background stories, courses, soundscapes, or podcast episodes — you can license that content to other creators, platforms, or businesses. This turns your content into intellectual property (IP) that continues to earn money in the background. For example, you could license a bundle of guided meditations to a wellness app, license a podcast series to a streaming platform, or sell limited-use commercial rights to your audio lessons or narrations.

Sites like **AudioJungle**, **Envato Elements**, **Pond5**, and even **Gumroad** can be used to sell licenses to audio assets. You can set your own terms: personal use, commercial use, exclusive or non-exclusive. Even your cloned voice (if allowed by platform policy) can be licensed to clients who want a specific style or tone in their audio projects. This model opens the door to scalable, high-ticket deals without constant production work.

To summarize, scaling your AI voice business means going beyond simple narration. Use **voice cloning** to personalize and streamline your content creation. Use **multilingual narration** to tap into new audiences around the world. And use **licensing models** to turn your voice content into sellable, repeatable digital assets. This is how you move from being a solo creator to building a scalable, voice-powered brand.

Next, let's dive into the story of an artist who went from selling a single AI-narrated meditation to licensing her entire voice content library to wellness companies — in three different languages.

Amara was making passive income doing what she loved

Amara Lopez had always been a creative soul — a visual artist, yoga teacher, and part-time wellness blogger. But what she loved most was writing meditations. She would spend early mornings crafting poetic, peaceful scripts meant to calm the mind and connect with the breath. One day, a student in her yoga class asked if she had audio recordings of her meditations. Amara hesitated. "No, but... I've thought about it." That night, she decided to make one.

She didn't have a good mic or a quiet recording space. But she had recently read about AI voices that sounded human and peaceful. She signed up for ElevenLabs, pasted her script into the editor, and chose a soft, breathy female voice. The result was stunning. She closed her eyes and listened — it felt like her words had come to life through someone else. She added soft music from a royalty-free library, uploaded the meditation to YouTube, and titled it "Morning Grounding Practice." Within a week, it had 2,000 views.

That single video inspired a wave of content. Amara wrote ten new meditations — each focused on a theme like gratitude, energy, or inner peace — and narrated them using her favorite AI voice. She bundled the audio tracks into a digital album and sold it on Gumroad for $19. People loved it. Reviews poured in. "So soothing," "Feels like you're right here," "Better than Headspace." She was making passive income doing what she loved — without ever recording her own voice.

Then one customer messaged her in Spanish: "¿Tienes estas meditaciones en español?" Amara didn't — but the idea stayed with her. She used DeepL to translate her scripts, then went to PlayHT and selected a soft, native Spanish voice. The result felt just as calming. She released the Spanish version of her meditation pack. Sales doubled. She added French and Portuguese versions. Each new language opened doors to new customers. Her inbox was filled with thank-you notes from around the world.

But the real turning point came when a wellness app discovered her work on YouTube. They asked to license five of her meditations for $1,500 — non-exclusive, with attribution. She agreed. Then another app reached out. And a spa chain in Australia. She created a media kit, set licensing terms ($99 personal use, $199 commercial use, $1,000 exclusive), and began getting inquiries weekly.

Soon, Amara wasn't just creating meditations — she was running a content licensing business. She hired a freelancer to translate and format her scripts, and used voice cloning to create a unique voice that became her brand's identity. It was calm, feminine, and gently accented — just like her dream narrator. She expanded into soundscapes, affirmations, and sleep stories. Everything was powered by AI voices — but guided by her own creativity and message.

Amara's journey from artist to entrepreneur wasn't traditional. She didn't chase fame, go viral, or even speak on camera. She simply scaled what she loved with the help of technology. Today, her voice content plays in spas, apps, and playlists across five continents — and none of it required a microphone.

Her story is proof that when passion meets systems — and voice meets scale — you don't just create income. You create impact.

Chapter 8: Legal, Ethical, and Branding Considerations With AI Voices

As you grow your AI voice content business, it becomes increasingly important to understand the legal, ethical, and branding aspects of what you're creating. While AI voices open up incredible opportunities for content creators, freelancers, and entrepreneurs, they also come with serious responsibilities. This chapter will help you navigate potential legal pitfalls, maintain ethical integrity, and build a brand that's trusted and respected — even when the voice behind it isn't real.

Let's begin with **legal considerations**. One of the most critical legal issues when using AI voice tools is **usage rights**. Not all platforms allow commercial use of their voices on all plans. Some restrict use to personal projects unless you subscribe to a commercial or enterprise license. For example, ElevenLabs, PlayHT, and Murf have commercial usage tiers, and publishing or selling AI-generated audio using their voices without the appropriate license can lead to content takedowns, legal notices, or even account bans. Before selling audiobooks, freelance voiceover gigs, or course narration, check that your voice tool's terms of service explicitly allow it.

Closely tied to this is the issue of **voice cloning legality**. Creating a cloned voice of yourself is generally allowed — and in most cases, encouraged — as long as it's not used for deceptive purposes. However, cloning someone else's voice without permission is a violation of intellectual property and may result in legal action. Always obtain **written consent** if you plan to create or use another person's voice, even if they offer samples. Some tools require voice consent uploads to verify identity before allowing cloning. Do not use celebrity voices or well-known public figures unless explicitly licensed for impersonation or parody purposes under fair use — which is rarely the case commercially.

Another legal element to consider is **content ownership**. When using AI tools to generate voiceovers, you typically retain the copyright to the final audio product — provided you've created the text yourself and used a licensed voice for narration. However, you may not own the underlying voice model. This is important if you plan to resell the same audio across platforms or license it to third parties. If you're unsure about your rights, review the platform's FAQs and legal documentation, or contact their support before distributing your work at scale.

Now let's talk about **ethical considerations**. While the law defines what you can do, ethics define what you should do.

Misrepresenting AI voices as real humans — especially in customer-facing content — can damage trust. Be honest about your use of AI when appropriate. For example, instead of hiding that your course or audiobook is AI-narrated, you can mention that you've used cutting-edge voice technology to deliver a consistent, high-quality experience. This transparency often builds credibility and interest, especially in tech-savvy or entrepreneurial audiences.

Ethical use also includes how you market and distribute content. Don't falsely advertise your voiceovers as being performed by specific voice actors. Don't sell content you didn't create or heavily borrowed from other creators without transformation or permission. And don't use AI narration to create misleading or manipulative content, such as fake testimonials, false claims, or deceptive advertising. As AI regulation becomes more common, ethical violations can damage your brand or trigger legal scrutiny.

Now let's shift to **branding**. One of the biggest advantages of using AI voices is the ability to create a consistent, professional sound across all your content — without being tied to your own voice. You can use this to your advantage by creating a **branded voice identity**. Choose a voice style (calm, energetic, warm, confident, etc.), tone, and pacing that aligns with your message and audience. Use this same voice in your audiobooks, videos, podcasts, and ads to build familiarity and trust. Over time, people will recognize your content by its sound — just like they recognize a logo or jingle.

To reinforce your brand, give your AI voice a name (if it's a character), a backstory (for storytelling), or a role (like "Coach," "Narrator," "Host"). If you're cloning your own voice, that becomes even more powerful. Just be consistent. Branding also includes visual elements — match your voice tone with your colors, cover art, thumbnails, and typography. Whether you're calm and clean or bold and edgy, your brand should feel unified across platforms.

Finally, remember that your brand isn't just how your content sounds — it's how people **feel** about your work. If you position yourself as trustworthy, creative, and innovative — and consistently deliver value — your audience won't care whether the voice is synthetic or organic. They'll care that you helped them, moved them, educated them, or made them feel something.

In the next story, you'll meet a creator who went viral for using AI voices — but also faced backlash when he wasn't transparent. It's a lesson in how honesty, ethics, and branding go hand in hand when building a sustainable business in the age of AI.

Ethan's story

Ethan Ross wasn't trying to deceive anyone. When he started his faceless YouTube channel, it was just a side project — a way to share productivity tips he'd been journaling for years. He used an ElevenLabs voice because he didn't like how he sounded on camera. He kept his identity private, used stock footage, and posted every week. Within six months, his channel had exploded. One of his videos — "5 Habits That Changed My Life" — hit 1.2 million views. Subscribers poured in. Emails. Comments. Requests for coaching. People thought Ethan was a seasoned entrepreneur, a charismatic speaker with a buttery smooth voice.

He didn't correct them.

In fact, he leaned into the mystery. He created an online course using the same AI voice and branded it with a minimalist logo. People assumed he had recorded everything himself. His marketing language hinted at authenticity: "I'm sharing what's worked for me..." "You'll hear my journey..." It wasn't a lie — but it wasn't the full truth either. And eventually, someone noticed.

A viewer commented: "Is this voice AI? Sounds like ElevenLabs." Another followed up with a detailed thread on Reddit. A few fans defended him, saying the message mattered more than the voice. But others felt betrayed. "You made it seem like it was you," one user wrote. "If you'll lie about your voice, what else are you exaggerating?"

Ethan was stunned. He had built something real — valuable content, heartfelt scripts, helpful advice. But he hadn't been transparent, and now his brand was taking a hit. He posted a video titled "The Truth About My Voice." In it, he came clean: "Yes, I use AI voice technology. It allows me to focus on writing and strategy. The words are mine. The voice is a tool." He showed a behind-the-scenes clip of his workflow and explained why he started the channel in the first place.

The response was mixed — but ultimately positive. Subscribers appreciated the honesty. A few even praised the decision. "This makes me like your channel even more," one comment read. "Thanks for being real." Ethan updated his website and course descriptions to reflect the AI narration. He rebranded slightly — embracing the role of the writer-creator behind the machine voice. It wasn't perfect, but it was authentic. And it worked.

From then on, Ethan's brand became about transparency, innovation, and simplification. He released a series called "Creating With AI," where he shared how he used voice tools to scale content creation. He attracted a new audience — creators who didn't want to be on camera but still wanted to build something meaningful. His story was now a case study in ethics, branding, and trust.

He had learned the hard way that your voice — whether AI or real — carries weight. It becomes a symbol of your message. And if that message is built on truth, value, and consistency, it can grow into something powerful. Ethan didn't just recover — he grew. But only because he chose to lead with integrity.

Chapter 9: Using AI Voices to Build Authority, Influence, and a Long-Term Brand

Most people think of AI voices as tools — ways to save time, reduce costs, or automate tedious narration tasks. And they're right. But if you stop there, you'll miss one of the most powerful opportunities AI voice content can offer: the ability to **build long-term authority, influence, and a trusted brand**. In this chapter, we'll shift from monetization to brand positioning — and how to use your voice-powered content to lead a niche, teach at scale, and become a voice of value (even if it's not your own).

To build authority with AI voice content, the first step is **owning your message**. Authority doesn't come from sounding good — it comes from delivering value consistently. Whether you're narrating audiobooks, publishing podcast episodes, or producing faceless YouTube videos, the power is in what you say. That means choosing a focused niche, solving specific problems, and showing up with content that genuinely improves lives. Authority is earned through repetition, quality, and intention — not just volume.

Next is **consistency of presence**. When someone hears your AI-narrated voice across multiple platforms — your audiobook, YouTube channel, email series, and course — it creates the illusion of omnipresence. This builds familiarity, and familiarity builds trust. People start recognizing "your voice" even if they've never seen your face. To reinforce this, use the same narrator or AI voice persona across your content library. Build a branded intro/outro. Use the same music and structure in your podcasts and videos. Over time, your AI voice becomes your signature.

One way to amplify this authority is by **teaching at scale**. Digital courses, AI-narrated tutorials, and value-packed audiobooks allow you to educate thousands of people with the same content. As your voice teaches people — especially in evergreen formats — it positions you as a leader in your field. Add downloadable resources, follow-up checklists, and bonus content to increase engagement and perceived value. Promote your voice-powered content as the first step in a learning journey — then build funnels into coaching, memberships, or communities.

You also build influence by **embedding your voice in other ecosystems**. For example, licensing your audio content to creators, apps, or educators in your niche helps you reach new audiences. You can collaborate with influencers by offering AI voice versions of their scripts, meditations, or newsletters. If you're in health, finance, real estate, or business, your AI voice content can power podcasts, online academies, and even explainer apps. This helps you go from solo creator to digital leader — the go-to voice for a topic or transformation.

Another key to long-term brand building is **storytelling**. Humans don't just remember facts — they remember stories. Infuse your AI voice content with stories from your life, your audience, or relevant case studies. Even if you're using AI, your content should sound like it came from real experiences. That's what makes people feel connected. When people say things like "I feel like I know you" after listening to your content, you're doing it right. Your voice becomes a channel for trust, transformation, and emotional resonance.

Finally, **elevate your brand with thought leadership**. Share bold insights, challenge assumptions, and deliver unique frameworks or philosophies through your content. This separates you from content farms and generic narrations. If your AI voice is consistently tied to powerful ideas — not just products — you'll build a brand that stands the test of time. Use your platform to teach, yes — but also to lead. That's how brands like Tim Ferriss, Brené Brown, or Naval Ravikant emerged: by showing up with ideas, clarity, and courage — consistently.

So don't just use AI voice content to "get by." Use it to **become the voice people trust**. Whether it's 100 followers or 100,000 students, your audience will remember how your content made them feel. And that feeling — that trust — is your most valuable asset.

Now, let's step into the story of a wellness expert who used AI narration not just to educate her audience — but to lead a global movement around healing and emotional freedom.

5 Minutes to Emotional Calm

Layla Shah was a licensed therapist who had always struggled with visibility. Her private practice was thriving locally, but deep down, she wanted to reach more people. "There are too many people suffering in silence," she often said. She had ideas, frameworks, and tools — but no platform. She tried blogging. No traction. She posted on Instagram. Minimal engagement. Then a friend sent her a voice-narrated YouTube meditation and said, "You could totally do something like this — your work is amazing." That suggestion changed everything.

Layla wrote a simple script titled, "5 Minutes to Emotional Calm." She used ChatGPT to help her format it like a short meditation, then logged into ElevenLabs. She chose a warm, nurturing female voice that reminded her of how she spoke to clients. She generated the audio, added soft background music, and uploaded it to YouTube with the title: “Daily Grounding Practice for Anxiety.” She didn’t expect much.

A week later, the video had 12,000 views. The comments blew her away. “This saved me today.” “I needed this more than you know.” “Subscribed instantly.” She had finally found her voice — even if it wasn’t hers. And it gave her the confidence to do more.

Layla started narrating short versions of the tools she used in therapy. Grounding techniques. Emotional release exercises. Trauma education. All written by her, voiced by AI, and delivered with love. She created a podcast called “The Self-Soothing Library.” She turned her scripts into an audiobook called *Healing in Your Hands*. She launched a Gumroad course that combined AI-narrated audio with downloadable workbooks.

But what surprised her the most was how people responded to the voice. “I feel safe listening to this.” “Who is the narrator? She’s amazing.” Layla smiled every time. “That’s my message — just a little help from technology.” She wasn’t hiding anything — in fact, she started showing her workflow on

Instagram, where therapists and coaches began asking how they could do the same.

Before long, Layla was teaching other mental health professionals how to scale their impact with AI voices. She created a membership site, narrated by AI, teaching them how to write scripts, generate voiceovers, and package their work into healing audio. She was no longer just a therapist — she was a mentor, an educator, and a movement builder.

Her voice — or rather, the digital extension of her voice — became her brand. Consistent, compassionate, clear. People followed her not just for the content, but for the calm it brought. They trusted her. And that trust turned into books, speaking invitations, and international licensing deals with mental health platforms.

Layla never expected to build a global brand. She just wanted to help more people. But by showing up with intention, by embracing AI as a bridge — not a mask — she became a voice of healing for thousands. And she did it not by shouting louder, but by speaking consistently, with purpose and love.

Chapter 10: Your Next Steps — Launching and Growing Your Voice Content Business

You've now explored the full potential of AI voice technology — from creating audiobooks and podcasts to selling voiceover gigs, launching faceless YouTube channels, and scaling your content into a global brand. Whether you're just starting out or already earning income, the final chapter of this journey is about taking action, launching confidently, and growing with intention. In this chapter, we'll map out your next steps to turn knowledge into momentum and create a sustainable, income-generating voice content business powered by AI.

The first step is to **pick a focus area**. While AI voices can be used in countless ways, success comes faster when you start with a single use case. Choose the one that fits your current strengths or assets. If you already have a blog or book, begin by turning it into an audiobook. If you're active on social media, start a faceless video channel using narrated scripts. If you're skilled at writing and organizing ideas, launch a voice-narrated course. The most profitable creators don't try to do everything at once — they build one thing well, then repurpose it later.

Next, **design your first monetized product or channel**. If you're creating an audiobook, format your manuscript, generate audio chapter by chapter, and upload it to Findaway Voices or ACX. If you're launching a YouTube channel, create a video script, generate a voiceover, match it with visuals, and publish with optimized titles and thumbnails. If you're building a course, record lessons using AI voice and slides, then publish to platforms like Udemy or Teachable. Choose a name, brand identity, and create a simple landing page or bio link where people can access everything you offer.

Once you've launched, focus on **building momentum through consistency**. That could mean publishing one audiobook per month, one podcast per week, or one YouTube video every three days. AI gives you speed and leverage — use it to outpace your competition without sacrificing quality. Set up templates and workflows. Keep your voice consistent. Repurpose your content across formats to maximize reach. Your goal isn't perfection — it's persistence. With each post, you're building trust, discoverability, and brand recognition.

As you grow, prioritize **audience building and list growth**. Use your content to drive email subscribers or followers to a central hub — a newsletter, Discord server, private podcast feed, or community. This is where you'll announce new releases, get early feedback, and drive sales without relying on algorithms. Add calls-to-action in your AI-narrated content — things like, "Subscribe to get the next episode," or "Download the free guide in the description." Even if your voice is AI, your engagement should be real and human.

Don't forget to **diversify your income streams**. Once you've built one profitable system, add others slowly. For example, if your podcast is doing well, bundle your scripts into an ebook or course. If your audiobook is selling, license it in other languages. If your YouTube channel has traffic, add affiliate links, sponsorships, or a digital product store. Let your content feed your business. Build a library, not just a few files.

Finally, **plan for scale**. That means documenting your workflows, using automation platforms like Zapier or Make.com, and hiring help when needed. If you're earning income from audiobooks, hire a VA to format manuscripts. If you're producing weekly content, outsource research or thumbnails. The goal isn't to do more — it's to do less, better. Create systems so you can focus on vision, creativity, and growth.

Your journey doesn't end here — this is the beginning. AI voice content isn't just a trend. It's a transformation. The ability to speak to the world — instantly, repeatedly, and without limits — is now in your hands. You don't need to be famous. You don't need to be extroverted. You don't even need a microphone. All you need is your voice — your message — and a system that lets it be heard.

Now, let's close with a final story — one that shows what's possible when someone steps fully into this opportunity and builds a business, brand, and legacy using nothing but AI and the courage to create.

How Tyler created Brain Fuel

Tyler Brooks wasn't looking for a business. He just wanted out of the grind. A former schoolteacher, he had burned out after ten years of juggling grading papers, after-school meetings, and rising classroom sizes. He loved teaching — just not the system. One summer, after quitting his job, he found himself searching YouTube for side hustles. He watched a video titled "Make $100/Day With AI Voice Content." At first, he rolled his eyes. But something stuck. "I know how to teach. I just don't want to be on camera." That was the seed.

Tyler wrote a short script: "How to Learn Anything Faster." It was based on a workshop he used to teach. He fed it into ElevenLabs, chose a warm male narrator, and generated the voiceover. He added slides in Canva, created a basic video in Pictory, and uploaded it to YouTube. The video got 56 views in three days. He almost gave up. But then a comment appeared: "This is gold. Please do more like this."

Encouraged, Tyler wrote four more scripts. One on memory, one on focus, one on note-taking, and one on learning styles. He created a mini-course called *Smart Learning Toolkit*, voiced entirely with AI. He listed it on Gumroad for $17 and offered a free audio lesson in exchange for an email. Within a month, he had 150 subscribers and 30 sales. Not life-changing — but real. Proof of concept.

He doubled down. He turned each module into a YouTube video. He compiled the scripts into an audiobook. He started a podcast called *Brain Fuel*, where he released weekly five-minute learning tips — all AI-narrated. He used ConvertKit to email his list weekly and added links to his products, new content, and even affiliate tools for learners. His income grew from $300/month to $2,000/month in three months.

Tyler realized the power wasn't just in the tools — it was in his message. He wasn't just publishing AI voice content. He was helping people learn better. He was still a teacher — just with more reach, freedom, and creativity than ever before. By year one, he had released six audiobooks, five mini-courses, and 100+ pieces of narrated content. His YouTube channel passed

10,000 subscribers. His email list topped 5,000. And his business passed $10K/month in income.

But most importantly, he was proud again. Proud of his voice — even if it was AI-generated. Proud of the learners he reached. Proud that he didn't stay stuck.

Tyler's story is a reminder: the tools are here. The market is ready. The only thing missing is your decision to begin.

Epilogue: AI is your vessel

We've reached the end of this book, but in truth, this is only the beginning. What you've explored here is not just a guide—it's a gateway. A gateway to a new era where technology no longer replaces creativity, but enhances it. Where artificial intelligence—once reserved for research labs and science fiction—is now your partner in expression, growth, and income. You've witnessed how a simple block of text can be transformed into powerful audio that moves people, teaches skills, or tells stories. And more importantly, you've seen how that transformation can be monetized, scaled, and personalized.

From the early chapters, you learned how the voiceover industry has evolved. You now know the difference between robotic text-to-speech and emotionally rich AI narration. You've discovered platforms that can clone your voice, read in multiple languages, adjust tone and pacing, and even carry your words to audiences in countries you may never visit. And the best part? These tools are no longer hidden behind expensive paywalls or reserved for elite media companies. They're available to you right now, often for free or at minimal cost. Your limitations no longer lie in access—they lie only in imagination and execution.

This book isn't just a manual. It's a map. A map that can guide a teacher to global impact without needing a classroom. A freelancer to consistent income without owning a microphone. A writer to audience-wide influence without ever stepping on a stage. The tools we've discussed are democratizing storytelling, education, and entrepreneurship. Whether you're in a quiet apartment or a noisy home, whether you're tech-savvy or brand new to this world, you now have everything you need to build something powerful. The tools are here. The marketplace is ready. The opportunity is massive.

But remember: tools are only as powerful as the people who use them. The AI-generated voice is just a vessel. What gives it meaning, what gives it weight and depth, is *you*. Your ideas. Your passion. Your story. It's your creativity and your perspective that turn synthetic voices into human connection. That's the secret most people miss. Technology alone isn't transformative—*creators* are. You are. What you say, what you share, what you teach—those are the things that matter. The voice is simply how it travels.

So, what now? Now is the time to build. Record that first narrated article. Repurpose a blog post into an audiobook sample. Launch a gig offering AI voiceovers for businesses. Narrate your course, translate it into five languages, and upload it to global platforms. Begin small, but start smart. Test everything. Learn fast. Iterate often. Don't wait until it's perfect—because it never will be. The creators who win in this new era aren't the ones with the best gear—they're the ones with the best *momentum*.

And as you move forward, never forget the values that guide long-term success: transparency, consistency, creativity, and a willingness to serve. Whether you're telling stories, teaching skills, or building a business—your impact is measured by how well you help others. Profit follows value. And value starts with intention.

The future belongs to those who adapt. To those who blend old-school work ethic with new-school tools. To those who stop asking for permission and start publishing, sharing, shipping, selling. You don't need to be famous. You don't need to be loud. You don't even need to be seen. All you need is a system, a story, and a strategy—and now, you have all three. That's the power of the AI voiceover revolution.

So keep learning. Keep creating. Keep testing, tweaking, and growing. Whether your first project is a narrated social media post or a meditation voiceover—you are laying the foundation for something scalable, profitable, and meaningful. And as the tools evolve, so will you.

Thank you for joining me on this journey. Thank you for believing in your voice—whether recorded, generated, or somewhere in between. The world is listening. It's time to give your words a voice. And your voice? It's time to give it a legacy.

www.ingramcontent.com/pod-product-compliance
Lightning Source LLC
LaVergne TN
LVHW022021200926
848481LV00007B/2473
9798349630729